"GOD, HELP ME"

D0721086

"God, Help Me"

Short Prayers for Busy Women

Harriet Crosby

**Andrews McMeel
Publishing**

Kansas City

www.andrewsmcmeel.com

99 00 01 02 03 BIN 10 9 8 7 6 5 4 3 2 1

Library of Congress Cataloging-in-Publication Data
Crosby, Harriet.
   God, help me : short prayers for busy woman / Harriet Crosby.
      p.   cm
   ISBN 0-8362-7857-7 (pbk.)
   1. Christian women—Prayer-books and devotions—English.
I. Title.
BV4844.C697 1999
242'.843—dc21   98-53693
                                                            CIP

Design by Holly Camerlinck

FOR GEORGE LEIS, WHO LIKES
TO SEE HIS NAME IN PRINT

Contents

INTRODUCTION

A Book for Full-time Marthas and Part-time Marys

I open my day-planner calendar to review today's schedule. It's going to be a busy Friday: Four meetings at work this morning, and a project deadline to meet by two o'clock. Rush home and take the cats to the vet for their annual vaccinations. Straighten up the house. Make dinner for four people and entertain them throughout the evening. And I see Saturday isn't much better—in addition to spending time with various friends and family, I've got a list of errands and chores to do that's longer than my arm.

Martha is a terrific Christian. She does everything right. She welcomes Jesus into her home and offers him hospitality to make him comfortable. Who can blame her if she gets just a bit frazzled, what with doing this and that with no help at all? Meanwhile, Martha's sister, Mary, sits all dreamy-eyed, resting at Jesus' feet, doing nothing but hanging on his every word. Jesus seems to be enjoying himself immensely. So Martha takes a small shot at Mary through Jesus: "Lord, do you not care that my sister has left me to do all the work by myself? Tell her then to help me." Lord, do you not care . . . ? Martha's shot hit the bull's eye, and Jesus feels the sting of her words. With boundless tenderness he looks straight into Martha's anxious heart. After a long silence, Jesus almost whispers, "Martha, Martha, you are worried and distracted by many things; there is need of only one thing. Mary has chosen the better part, which will not be taken away from her."

Mary is a mystic. She chose "the better part," to sit quietly at Jesus' feet, gaze on him, and contemplate his words. She is quiet. Rarely does Mary say a word. I've always imagined Mary as a woman who led a lively spiritual life on the inside, invisible to all but God.

Martha's spiritual life is lived very much on the outside. She follows the ancient Jewish practice of hospitality.

She is outspoken, telling Jesus exactly what's on her mind. She is pragmatic and down-to-earth (later, at the death of her brother Lazarus, Martha cautions Jesus against the stench that surely fills the tomb). Notice that Jesus does not condemn Martha or her hospitable efforts. Martha isn't doing anything wrong. She is in no way inferior to her sister, Mary. Jesus simply points out that only "one thing" is needed— to listen to his words.

Most of us are full-time Marthas and part-time Marys. While there are certainly some rare times of rest and contemplation in our lives, most of us are called to be busy women like Martha. We have jobs to do, families to raise, church or community responsibilities. God calls us to these things as surely as Mary was called to sit at Jesus' feet.

And yet, busy Marthas that we are, we each feel the stirrings of Mary inside us too. It's no accident that these very different women are related by blood. As sisters, each complements the other. Jesus enjoys the friendship of both. They represent two sides of the spiritual life: a life devoted to God in the world and a life devoted to God in the heart.

Again I look at my calendar. I envy Mary. But I celebrate Martha because God is calling me to this life, to my life, which is full-time and busy—and belongs to God. This book is for women like me, full-time Marthas and part-time Marys. The prayers in this book are for busy women whose hearts belong to God.

These prayers celebrate Martha while honoring Mary in each of us. In the midst of our busy days, we can let ourselves be Mary and hang on God's every word in prayer. But these prayers aren't reserved for quiet moments or times of serenity and inner peace. Sometimes our really heartfelt prayers are prayed when we are most overwhelmed, coping with some kind of crisis, or so busy we're just barely hanging in there. These prayers are to be prayed when we are right in the thick of our days and need a few words to give us the strength to do the next thing.

"God, Help Me" is designed to be carried with you in a

briefcase or purse. It contains
small prayers on a variety of
topics to use throughout the
day. These brief words let the
Mary in you strengthen the
Martha. Say them whenever
and wherever you choose,
alone or with others. There is
need of only one thing on this
busy day—pray.

HOURS AND DAYS

God,

There is never enough time.

Help me to make wise deci-

sions about how to spend it.

Guide me to use my time for

those things—and people—

that are most important to

me. Amen.

God,
I love you. Never forget that
I love you. No matter how
busy I am, I love you. I
thought you should know.
Amen.

God,

I need to spend time with

you. Help me to make sure

there's room for you in my

schedule. Amen.

God,

I just can't do everything.

Show me what I *can* do.

Show me what I need to let

go of and give me the

courage to walk away. Amen.

God,

My schedule is more than just
a list of appointments. My
schedule shows me what and
who is important to me. Help
me to organize my priorities.
Amen.

God,
This morning is so beautiful
and still. I hear the whisper of
your voice in the silence. I'm
glad you're here with me
now. Amen.

God,

There is not enough time in the morning. I have to get everybody else ready and out the door before I can get myself ready to go too. Help me to remember to talk with you first thing every morning. Amen.

God,

This morning promises a new
day filled with new begin-
nings. Help me not to waste
any opportunities to start
fresh. Open my eyes to see
open doors today. Amen.

God,

I want to crawl back into
bed. I just can't face another
day. Give me the strength I
need to work and to love.
Walk with me and let me
know that I don't go forth
into this day alone. Amen.

God,

The day is half over. Thank
you for all I've been able to
accomplish. Give me the
energy I need to finish the
day well. Amen.

God,

I'm too busy today to take
time for lunch. But I am
aware of your presence even
now. Thank you for standing
by me in this zoo. Amen.

God,
Thank you for this chance to
take a break in the afternoon.
I can catch my breath and tell
you that I love you. I love
you. Amen.

God,

Today has been such a gift. I

pause this afternoon to give

you thanks for work to do

and people to love—and for

the beauty of this day. Amen.

God,

The sun is setting and at last

I can look toward home. As

this day ends and work ceas-

es, help me to know that it's

you I come home to. Amen.

God,

I may be on my way home
from work now, but my sec-
ond job is about to begin.
Help me to get dinner, give
baths, make conversation, listen to my family. And after all
these things are done, help
me to get a little rest. Amen.

God,

The evening is so peaceful

and quiet. There's a very faint

glow in the sky where the sun

used to be. As the morning is

your creation, so is the

evening. All praise to you.

Amen.

God,

Thank you for the day that

has passed. Help me find you

in the night that is to come.

And when we meet, let me

know the power of your love.

Amen.

God,

Finally a little peace and
quiet. The house is still. I
hear only the sound of my
own breath. Thank you for
the quiet of this night and for
your presence in the darkness.
Amen.

God,

Protect all who live within
this house from the fears and
dangers of the night. Let
your presence shine quietly in
the dark. Bring us in safety to
a new day filled with the
hope of your love. Amen.

God,

Help me to get some sleep!

I'm so anxious and wound up

that I can't keep my eyes

closed. Relieve my worried

mind. Help me to rest in you.

Amen.

God,

I don't spend enough time

looking at the stars. Looking

at the stars tonight reminds

me that the most important

thing in the universe is love—

love of you, of family, of

friends. Help me never to

take love for granted. Amen.

God,

I look at the week ahead and
wonder how I'm going to get
through it. Help me not to
anticipate the days that lie
ahead but to live each one,
knowing that you walk with
me into the future. Amen.

God,

What a week! The weekend is
coming and I badly need a
little rest and recreation.
Help me to recover from
these five busy, tumultuous
days. Help me have a little
fun. Amen.

God,

How I wish I could live my
life on my own time instead
of living the days around the
work week and the school
week. But work and school
are here to stay for now. Help
me to find time for myself in
a week largely outside of my
control. Amen.

God,
Another month gone. The
season is beginning to
change. Help me to accept
the joys and challenges of the
coming month with grace
and peace. Amen.

God,

I just turned the page in my

calendar. What happened to

next month? There's too

much to do in too little time.

Help me not to waste the

coming days. Help me to

savor each one in spite of the

busyness. Amen.

God,

This month looks like it's
going to be a quiet one. Keep
me from filling up every day
with busyness. Help me to
leave plenty of time for doing
nothing at all. Amen.

God,

The thought of next year
overwhelms me. All the
birthdays and anniversaries,
annual checkups and reviews,
all the triumphs and all the
losses yet to be lived. Help
me to live each day one at a
time, relying on your love to
take care of me. Amen.

God,

Another year is gone. Am I
any wiser? Maybe a little. One
thing I know for sure: You
walked with me through
every hour of every day,
though I could not always
feel your presence. Thank you
for what has passed, and
thank you for what is to
come. Amen.

FAMILY AND FRIENDS

God,

Take care of my children

while I am away from them

today. Keep them safe; let

them know you are near. And

help me not to worry about

them. Amen.

God,

There are too many noisy

kids in this car pool and I

think I'm going to scream.

Form in me a place that's

quiet and let me walk with

you there, away from car

pools and traffic and kids.

Amen.

God,

Are you sure children are a
blessing? All the worry, late
nights, expense. But I've
never loved like this before;
they are more precious to me
than life itself. Thank you,
God, for my children. Amen.

God,
My kids are turning into
people! I wish I could go
with them everywhere and
protect them from all the bad
things that can happen in life.
But I can't. Give me the love
I need to let them go and
make their own way. Amen.

God,

The kids wanted dinner an hour ago, and I just got home. They're wild. You know what kind of day I've had. Give me the strength to provide for them as you provide for me. Amen.

God,

He can be a pain! But at least

he's *my* pain. Help me to love

him in spite of all the annoy-

ing little things he does.

Because I do love him and I

want to love him more.

Amen.

God,

Men. Who needs them? I do.

I don't like being alone just

now and could use some

male companionship. Would

you please send a little my

way? Amen.

God,

I didn't know I could love

someone so much. I didn't

know someone could love me

so much. Keep us in love, O

God, and guard our love

through thick and thin.

Amen.

God,

We're going through a tough time right now. We're traveling blind through a strange country. Help us both to find our way. And let us find you at the end of our journey.

Amen.

God,

It's just another ordinary day.

But I am so grateful, O God,

for my helper, friend, and

lover. Never let me take him

for granted. Amen.

God,

You know my parents drive

me crazy. Be with me while

I'm with them. Grant me the

serenity I need to honor

them. Amen.

God,

I still love my parents with a

child's love. I know you love

them even more than I do.

Take care of them and keep

them in the palm of your

hand. Amen.

God,

Show me how to love my

parents today. Help me to be

my best with them. And keep

me from taking them for

granted. Amen.

God,

I miss my parents and wish
they were here. Keep me
company in their absence and
help me to remember that
you are my heavenly parent.
Amen.

God,

Help me in my role as

daughter-in-law. Guide me

and direct me in my relation-

ship with my in-laws and help

me to see the light of your

love in their eyes. Amen.

God,
Give me strength. It's time
for the in-laws. Help me to
deal with them with dignity
and respect. Amen.

God,

Thank you for my in-laws, for
their love and care. I couldn't
ask for better parents. I'm
glad they are family. Amen.

God,

Thank you for my family.

Loving them isn't always easy.

But sometimes, when I look

in their eyes, I see you look-

ing out at me, and I tremble

with love for them. Thank

you. Amen.

God,

Thank you for friends. I can

trust in your goodness and

mercy because you've

brought them into my life.

Bless our friendship and help

it to grow and deepen.

Amen.

God,

I could use a few friends right

now. Everything feels strange

and uncertain. Friendship is

such a great anchor. Please

send a friend my way. Amen.

God,

Help me to be the kind of
friend I would want to have.
Strengthen my loyalty in the
relationship through fair
weather and foul. And let us
always find joy and delight in
each other. Amen.

God,

Sometimes when the going

gets tough, a few good

friends are hard to find. Show

me who my real friends are.

Let me lean on the strength

of their love. Amen.

God,

It's so hard to say good-bye!
Help us find a way to main-
tain our friendship across the
miles that separate us. Amen.

God,

My pet may not be human,

but she is a true friend.

Thank you, God, for such a

faithful, loyal companion. I

love her very much. Amen.

God,

You are the Creator of all
creatures, great and small.
Keep my furry friend in good
health. May she always be
playful and happy, get plenty
to eat, and have lots of naps
in the sun. Amen.

God,

_____ is sick. Let him

know your healing touch.

Hold him in the palm of your

hand. Help me to make the

best decisions I can about his

care. Amen.

PEACE AND SERENITY

God,

It's easy to love my family
and friends when times are
good and things are going
well. Help me to love them
when the going gets tough—
like right now. Teach me to
love them as you love them:
freely, expecting nothing in
return. Amen.

God,

I don't love _____ right
now. But I want to love her
in spite of what I don't feel.
Give me the courage and
grace to love even though I
don't feel like it. Amen.

God,

I don't know why you love

me—but you do. Your love

for me is a complete mystery.

Help me give up trying to

understand or rationalize

your love; help me to accept

it as a fabulous gift. Amen.

God,

Thank you for this life, for all you've given me to do, for all the people who both love and challenge me. I know you speak to me in this life in every moment of every day. Give me ears to hear your voice. Amen.

God,

Simple kindness doesn't get a
lot of press these days. But I
sure could use a little right
now. Show me some kindness
today. And help me to pass a
little of your kindness along
to someone else. Amen.

God,

I'm sick and tired of beating

myself up. I wouldn't treat

my dog the way I treat

myself. Help me to show

some kindness to myself

today. Help me to lighten

up—and let in your love.

Amen.

God,

Strangers scare me. But I

know that not all strangers

want to hurt me. Help me be

a little kinder to people I

don't know—for I may some-

day be kind to an angel in

disguise. Amen.

God,

Help me to be faithful to the
people who matter most—my
family and friends. Let me
show them that they can
depend on me for love no
matter what. Help my love to
be like yours, solid and
unchanging. Amen.

God,

Your faithfulness to me is beyond measure. I look back over my life and cannot count how many times your hand has been upon me to provide for me, strengthen me, love me. To you I give all my thanks. Amen.

God,

This is a faithless world.

Loyalties and allegiances

change and shift from

moment to moment. Love

that was here yesterday is

gone tomorrow. But you, O

God, are my rock; your faith-

fulness toward me is

unchanging. Help me to lean

on your faithfulness now.

Amen.

God,

There is so much going on

today that I've lost sight of

you. But I know even now

you shadow my every step.

Give me the strength I need

to trust that you are with me

even though the clamor of

events and people may seem

to keep you away. Amen.

God,

You promise me peace. I
believe you can deliver on
your promise. Help me to
find something of your peace
today. Amen.

God,

I am not a naturally calm person. I need your help. Help
me to rest—if only for a few
minutes today—in your
peace. Amen.

God,

I'm asking for a miracle.

When friends, colleagues, and

family see me today, let them

see your peace in me. For I

know that peacemakers are

blessed. Amen.

God,

Help me to be generous with

more than just my money.

Give to me a generous spirit.

Help me to give myself away

more often. Amen.

God,

I know you are pleased with a generous spirit. Help me to be generous with love and acceptance—of myself and others. Amen.

God,

Help me to know that there

is enough and more than

enough of your love to go

around. Let me be generous

with your love toward

whomever I meet today.

Amen.

CAREER AND WORK

God,

I hear you calling me to be a

_____. Give me the

patience and strength to fol-

low my vocation. Guide my

footsteps to become the one

you are calling me to be.

Amen.

God,

I thank you that my job is my
vocation. For this blessing I
am truly grateful. I am grateful that your hand is upon
me, and that you give me the
grace to do my work with joy.
Amen.

God,

I may not get paid for it, but

you've given me a passion for

_____. For the joy it

brings to me and others, I am

very grateful. Help me to

grow and flourish in my craft,

that I may always delight in

it. Amen.

God,

The time I can spend working on my _____ is holy
time. Let me always know
that to work at this is to wor-
ship you. For this sacred time
I offer thanks. Amen.

God,
All work, when dedicated and
offered to you, is holy. It
might be just a job—but I
dedicate it to you, that I may
find you today at work. I
offer my job to you, that I
may work your will. Amen.

God,

I hate my job. But I need it.
See me through today, and
keep me from doing some-
thing stupid. Help me come
another step closer to finding
other work that better suits
me. Amen.

God,

I love my job. Thank you for

this rare blessing. In a world

where too many people's

work is drudgery, let me

never take my job for granted.

Amen.

God,
It's Monday and I hope I've
won the lottery. But I doubt
it. Give me the motivation,
strength, patience, and wisdom I need to do a good job,
today and throughout the
week. Amen.

God,

I know life isn't fair. But

sometimes life at work *really*

isn't fair. Give me the

strength to change the things

I can and the wisdom to

accept what I can't change.

And guide me with your

Spirit. Amen.

God,

Just because I'm retired

doesn't mean I don't work.

No matter how large or small

the tasks today, help me to do

them well. And let me have

fun while I'm at it. Amen.

God,

Retirement isn't all it's cracked up to be. Give me the blessing of doing something meaningful with the rest of my life. Let me enjoy you and this time we have together. Amen.

God,

Today is holy. I give you
thanks for this day. Keep me
from taking it for granted.
Let all I do today show forth
your glory. Amen.

God,
I need a job. Help me find
one. And until I find one,
give me all I need to live and
thrive. Amen.

God,

What am I going to do now?

Show me what kind of work

you want me to do. Give me

the courage to explore and

learn as much as I can about

what I am to do for a living.

Amen.

God,

Money is tight. I know

money isn't everything—but

it sure means a lot just now.

Help me with my finances.

And provide me with a job

that pays the bills. Amen.

God,

I love money. Keep me from
loving it too much. Give me
the courage and generosity of
heart to give some of it away
to those in need. Amen.

God,

All good gifts come from
you—even money. Help me
to be wise and generous in its
use. And help me always to
remember that you alone are
the source of my good for-
tune. Amen.

God,

Surely a little more money

than I have right now

couldn't hurt. Please. Amen.

God,

Help me to be a good stew-
ard of my money. Help me to
invest it wisely and spend it
honorably. Let there always
be enough to share with my
family and friends and those
in need. Amen.

God,

Open my mind. Help me to

greet new ideas with joy—

instead of seeing them as just

more things to remember.

May what I learn today shape

me in your image. Amen.

God,

Work, school, family, and
friends: There's too much to
juggle. Help me to focus and
concentrate on one thing at a
time. Help me to learn what
I need to learn in school
today. Amen.

God,

Thank you for the opportunity to learn. Help me not to waste today's opportunity. Make my mind like a sponge, absorbing new ideas and experiences to enrich my life. Amen.

God,

School is not easy for me. I
need you to help me through
classes today. Help me to
relax in your presence, knowing that you'll go to school
with me. Amen.

God,

It is such a privilege to volun-

teer. Help me to do good

work today. And help the

lives of all those I touch.

Amen.

God,

I love my work as a volunteer.

Help me to remember that

what I do will benefit not

only those with whom I

come in contact today, but

also people whose names I'll

never know. Amen.

God,

This is one of the few times I
can spend alone with you.
Guide my thoughts; let me
rest in your peace; strengthen
my heart for whatever comes
next. Amen.

God,

Thank you for today. Thank
you for the work you've
given me to do. Help me to
do my best and to remember
that, no matter what I do
today, you hold me in the
palm of your hand. Amen.

God,

As I approach the office,

strengthen me for the day

ahead. Help me to see your

hand at work in all I do.

Help me to see you in the

eyes of my co-workers. Let

this be a good day. Amen.

God,

To say that today stunk is an
understatement. Today, work
was rotten. But you know
that. Rebuild my spirit as I
journey home. Bless me with
a calmness I do not yet feel.
Amen.

God,

Thank you for the day that is
past. As I turn toward home,
help me to let go. Help me
to leave work thoughts, wor-
ries, and victories at the
office. Clear my mind to
know only your love. Amen.

God,

What an idiot! Help me with

my attitude toward my boss.

Help me to stop thinking of

him as an idiot and to see

that he is here to do a job

just like I am. Amen.

God,

Help me not to take my boss

for granted. Working for

_____ is a personal as well as

a professional joy. My boss is

a blessing sent by you. Many

thanks. Amen.

God,
Help me to see my boss as
you see her. Let me treat my
boss with dignity and respect
so that both of us can get on
with the job. Amen.

God,

They say American workers
like me are supposed to be
competitive. Help me to
compete in a healthy way.
Keep me from feelings of
professional jealousy or envy
so that together my col-
leagues and I can do good
work. Amen.

God,

I have a responsibility to my staff to be the best leader and mentor I can be. That's a pretty tall order. I can't do it all alone. Help me to be a good, fair boss. Amen.

God,

There's so much to do today.
I know you will be at work
among us. Help me to moti-
vate and lead my staff so we
can all get our work done on
time and within budget.
Amen.

God,
I hate managing people.
_____ has been such a
pain. I've got to talk to him.
Help me to be fair, cool, and
clear as we talk. Amen.

God,

I've got the best staff in the
world. And I know each and
every one of them is a gift
from you. Thank you, God.
Help me to never take them
for granted. Amen.

BODY AND HEALTH

God,
Look what that scale says!
Something must be done.
Help me to find and use a
diet that helps me control my
weight, yet doesn't subtract
from my joy in living. Amen.

God,

Help me to eat properly and
well. Help me to honor my
body by feeding it healthy
food. Help me to remember
that my body is a temple.
Amen.

God,

I'm losing weight from stress.
This is not good. Help me to
relax and find my balance
again. Help me let go of that
which I cannot control so I
can increase my appetite for
living. Amen.

God,
Too fat. Too thin. To hell
with it! Help me remember
that you love me just the way
I am. Let me know your loving presence deep in my
heart. Amen.

God,

Look at that great woman in

the mirror! I feel good today.

I'm going to knock 'em dead!

Thank you, God, for this

beautiful feeling. Amen.

God,

Too often I wonder whether

I'm loved for my appearance.

I want to be loved for who I

am inside. Help me to know

that I am loved for the beauty

of my spirit. Amen.

God,

I'm afraid of getting older.
I'm afraid he won't love me
anymore. I'm afraid of one
day losing my job because I
am no longer young. Help
me to trust in your love and
care instead of youth and
beauty. For I know you love
me as I am. Amen.

God,
It's clear I'm getting older.
Once-firm muscles are sag-
ging a little. Help me to
grow old gracefully—to
accept and love my aging
body. Amen.

God,

I hate getting old. I hate not
being able to do everything I
used to do. I hate looking in
the mirror. Help me not to
hate growing old anymore.
Help me find a place of
serenity about aging. Amen.

God,

It's great being an "older person." At last I can do what I want without much concern about what others think of me. Help me to use my freedom wisely, that I may love and live well. Amen.

God,

I've been expecting this. I

didn't expect how big a

change it would be, though.

Help me walk through this

time in my life carefully, one

step at a time. Let me learn

to love the person I am

becoming. Amen.

God,

Menopause is wild! I don't know how I'm going to feel from one minute to the next. As I journey throughout this part of my life, help me to experience your faithfulness. Let me know that you never change. Amen.

God,

I feel like everybody's looking
at me differently. Yet I know
the real issue is that I need to
look at myself differently as I
go through menopause. Help
me to love the person I come
to see. Amen.

God,

I'm pregnant! I could burst
with joy! I have no words to
tell you how I feel—only that
I am so deeply grateful for
the gift of this child. Amen.

God,

I'm pregnant! This is not
supposed to happen. I'm ter-
rified beyond words. What
am I going to do? Show me a
way. Amen.

God,

Help this child grow strong

and sound within me.

Surround my baby with your

love as I surround my baby

with my body. For I know

you hold us both in the palm

of your hand. Amen.

God,

Pregnancy is not unending
bliss. I feel rotten. My ankles
are swollen. I'm enormous—I
have trouble getting up from
the couch. I'm exhausted.
Please let this baby come
soon! Amen.

God,

I hate you. I hate everybody.

I know my hormones are on

a rampage, but today I hate

the world. There's nothing

you or I can do. Just go away.

Amen.

PMS

God,

The "curse" isn't menstrua-
tion, it's PMS. Everybody's
steering clear of me. I feel
lonely and a little pissed off.
Keep me company for a
while. Amen.

God,

Help me to manage my emo-
tions in spite of my hormones
today. Help me to remember
to breathe slowly and deeply
to avoid getting uptight.
Help me to remember that
you love me just as I am.
Amen.

PMS

HOME AND GARDEN

God,
My garden makes my heart
sing your praises. I give you
thanks for the abundant life
all around me, especially my
plants. Let my thanks be as
pleasing to you as birdsong.
Amen.

God,

This winter's day, let my garden sleep in peace. As it sleeps, help prepare it for a glorious spring. And let me dream of new life during this winter's night. Amen.

God,

Help my garden produce
grow full and healthy. Defend
it from birds and insects that
would destroy it. Give me the
patience and diligence I need
to tend my garden for an
abundant harvest. Amen.

God,

Bless the earth in which my
garden grows. Bless all the
plants and flowers and veg-
etables that grow there. May
the rains be gentle and the
sun shine on it warmly.
Amen.

God,

It's good to be home. I hope heaven is like this—that comforting feeling of homecoming after work is through, to find your welcoming arms on just the other side of the front door. Amen.

God,

Bless this room that holds
family and friends. Let it be a
place of peace and harmony, a
place where we can enjoy and
love one another. Let it be a
place of comfort and recreation. Amen.

God,

So much living has been done
in this room. Heal any discord that has happened here.
Mend any hearts that have
been broken here. Let your
spirit live here among us.
Amen.

God,

May this room be filled with
welcome from a busy and
noisy world. Let all hearts
who enter here find warmth,
comfort, and healing. Let all
hearts who enter here find
you. Amen.

God,

May all who eat at this table
remember that the meals
served here come from your
hand. Help us to be always
grateful for our daily bread
and to use it to sustain our
bodies and our minds. Amen.

God,

Let this room be a place

where we perpetually offer

you our thanks. For all good

things, O God, come from

your hand. Whenever family

and friends enter here, create

in us grateful and loving

hearts. Amen.

God,

May all who join around this
table put away the cares and
troubles of the world so that
we may find you among us.
As we humbly eat of the food
you provide, put away from
us all discord and struggle.
And let us rejoice in each
other, in the food before us,
and in your presence. Amen.

God,

This is the best room. My
kitchen is the heart of our
house. May it always be warm
and welcoming and filled
with good things. Amen.

God,
This house is a zoo. There's
so much going on, running
in and out, so much to do.
Help me to be a still point in
my kitchen; let me know your
peace. Amen.

God,

I don't want to cook tonight.

But others are depending on

me. Give me strength. Help

me figure out something

that's good—and quick.

Amen.

God,

After the day I've had, going
to bed feels so good. Surely
this is the best time of day.
Help my body and mind relax
in your presence with me this
night. And let me awake in
the morning refreshed and
ready to go. Amen.

God,

This room is not only a place
to rest but also a place to
love. Help me to be a good
lover, that I may honor and
love my partner with my
body as well as my heart.
Amen.

God,

It's 2 A.M. and I'm so tense

and anxious I feel like I'm

levitating three feet above the

bed. Calm my mind; soothe

my body. Help me to relax

into the comfort of the mat-

tress, the soft warmth of the

blankets. Help me get some

sleep. Amen.

God,

It's so lonely to be in bed
with someone when love is
gone. What am I going to
do? Show me a way out. And
for this night, help me to
rest, somehow, in you. Amen.

God,

Look at them. They finally
crashed. They're such angels
when they're asleep. Bless
them and keep them safe
throughout the night in this
room. Amen.

God,

What's going on in there? I
don't know which is worse,
too much quiet or too much
noise. Help me to respect my
children's privacy and yet
intervene when I must.
Amen.

God,
This is a room in which my
children will make memories.
Let it be filled with fun and
happiness. Help them to
grow up good and strong.
Amen.

God,

I love this room the best. It is
a place of my own where I
can read, think, and take care
of my own business. Help me
to grow and thrive here in all
that I do. Amen.

God,

I don't care about using this
room to study; I come here
for peace and quiet. In this
room I can hear myself think.
Help me to hear you speak-
ing to me as well. Amen.

God,

My study is filled with books.

Help me to listen carefully to

the writers as I read. Help me

never to lose that sense of

wonder that their books

inspire. Amen.

God,

When I shut the door to the bathroom, it becomes the one room in the house where my family can't follow me. Let me sit here quietly for a little while. Give me the strength and energy I need to love them when I come out. Amen.

God,
This bathtub is my sanctuary.
Help my body to relax in the
warm, fragrant water. Heal
my mind of the day's prob-
lems and traumas. Let the
only voice I hear be yours.
Amen.

God,

My first look in the bathroom
mirror this morning tells too
much truth. Help me to age
gracefully. Help me to accept
getting older and to relax
into this body you've given
me. Amen.

God,

There's so much junk in here.

It reminds me how needlessly

complicated my life can be.

Help me to discern what I

really need to live well and to

let go of all the rest. Amen.

God,

I come here to look at the
memories. My life is rich and
full. Here, I am reminded of
your goodness toward me.
Thank you. Amen.

EARTH AND SKY

God,
Today is just gorgeous! The
sky is beautiful; the air is so
fresh that words fail me. All
praise to you, my Creator!
Amen.

God,
We need rain. Gardens and
crops are bone dry. Have
mercy on us and send the
rains. Heal the earth, your
creation. Amen.

God,

Last night's snowfall is beautiful. All is quiet, hushed by
the fresh snow. For winter's
beauty, I offer my thanks.
Amen.

God,

All this rain is driving me
crazy. It's dark all the time. It
wouldn't be so bad if I didn't
have to go out in it—but I
do. O God, how 'bout a little
break? Please send me a little
sunshine. Amen.

God,

I know you are much more

magnificent than the thunder.

But as the thunder claps over-

head, I'm reminded of you

and your greatness, your

power. And I am grateful that

you love me. Amen.

God,

I like walking with you. I put
one foot in front of the other
and feel the earth solid
beneath my feet. And I know
that your faithfulness toward
me is as solid as a rock.
Amen.

God,

The earth has suffered so
much at human hands. Help
me to do all I can every day,
in my small way, to preserve
the earth's resources and its
beauty. Use me to heal this
lovely planet. Amen.

God,

Digging in the earth is the
best therapy I know. I feel all
the tension flow from my
shoulders, down my arms,
and out of my fingertips, to
be buried in the soft, warm
soil. Help this earth, in which
I dig, to grow rich and
healthy flowers and plants.
Amen.

God,

Your voice is the sound of the
sea. As I listen to the crash of
the waves, help me to hear
you with my heart, mind, and
soul. Amen.

God,
The sea is so vast and I am so
small. Don't overlook me
here on the shore. Help me
to live courageously and to
love well. Amen.

CELEBRATIONS,
MILESTONES,
AND LIFE CHANGES

God,

Thank you for this life.

Thank you for the life of

_____. Bless to her this

day; may it be filled with joy

and delightful surprises.

Amen.

God,

You know how I love my

dear friend. Defend her from

all harm and sadness on this

her birthday. May she know

many more, each filled with

much love and good things.

Amen.

God,

Thank you for the gift of this
child. Bless him with love,
health, and happiness on this
birthday and all the birthdays
to come. And help me to sur-
vive the birthday party.
Amen.

God,

It's that time of year. There's

too much to do and I'm

already tired. As I prepare for

the holidays, help me to slow

down and remember you and

how much you love me.

Amen.

God,

This is my favorite time of

year. All the lights tell me

that your Light has come into

the world to live among us.

And I rejoice to give you

thanks and praise. Amen.

God,

Sometimes there doesn't

seem to be enough of any-

thing during the holidays—

not enough gifts or food or

happiness or love. Everybody

seems to want more and

more. Give to me the peace

of knowing that your love is

infinite and that you are

enough for me. Amen.

God,

In spite of all the people

around me, I am lonely this

holiday season. May I have

the honor of your company

and warm myself in the fire of

your love? Have mercy upon

me, O Lord. Amen.

God,

The hustle and bustle of the
holidays makes me feel so
good. I love the energy and
sense of great expectation.
Help me to slow down so I
don't miss a minute of it—
and so I don't miss the touch
of your grace. Amen.

God,

During this quiet moment in

the holiday season, let me

hear you whisper my name.

Let me know that your great

love for humanity includes

your particular love for me.

In silence, O God, I offer up

my love. Amen.

God,

May the joy that _____

and _____ experience

today strengthen and bind

them together as they journey

into the future. Let your

hand rest upon them this

day—and every day of their

life together. Amen.

God,

Only yesterday, he was a baby. Now he's getting married. Watch over and take care of my baby. He will need your love and care for the long journey ahead. Amen.

God,

Sometimes I didn't think we
were going to make it. But
by your grace and with your
help, we did. Thank you for
this marriage. Today let us
each see you in the other's
eyes. Amen.

God,

Through good times and

hard times your hand has

been upon _____ and

_____. Warm them

with memories of the past

and journey with them into

the future. Amen.

God,

Bless our marriage. Smile on
us and let us feel the warmth
of your love. Give me the
courage to love my partner
even more than I do today.
Amen.

God,

On this anniversary of my
divorce, heal any scars that
remain. Help me to let go of
the past so that I may walk
fearlessly into the future. And
let me know that you walk by
my side. Amen.

God,

Since my divorce you've been
making me into a new per-
son. It hasn't been easy. But I
know that my new life is in
your hands and ask that you
do with me according to your
will. Amen.

God,

I feel I've just lost a limb.

The divorce is final. The pain

is great; help me to bear it

well. Amen.

God,

The divorce is final and I am
free. Help me to use my new
freedom responsibly and with
love. Journey with me into a
future rich with possibilities.
Amen.

God,

I'm worried about the kids.

The divorce has hurt them

so. Hide them under the

shadow of your wings. Help

me to love them even more

than I do right now. Amen.

God,

Make me into a better

lover—physically, emotionally,

and spiritually. Help me to

learn more about love from

you. And give me the

courage to love fearlessly and

truthfully. Amen.

God,

I'm so anxious and worried I
feel I'm going to come
through my eyeballs. Yet I
know that all things rest in
the palm of your hand. Help
me to rest there too, calmed
by your love. Amen.

God,

I'm in love and I feel as if I
could kiss the whole world.
Thank you for the way I feel
today. Help me to stay in
love, and let me rejoice in
you, the Lover of my soul.
Amen.

God,

My heart is broken into so
many pieces that I doubt
even you can put it back
together again. Don't let me
give up on you. Mend my
heart, I pray, so that it is even
stronger than before. Amen.

God,

Deep sadness covers me and

darkness surrounds me. I can

barely get out of bed. Give

me strength. Rescue me from

this sadness; shine your light

into the darkness and lead me

back into life again. Amen.

God,

Save me from a life of fear.

Give me courage and peace

that comes from knowing

you walk beside me, even

when it feels like you're far

away. Be a present help to me

in this time of trouble. Amen.

God,

Life is good. I'm pretty happy

right now. Don't let me take

happiness for granted. Help

me to thank you every day

for this gift of happiness.

Amen.

God,

You are my joy. For you are

the giver of all good gifts and

the many blessings you shower

on me. Help me to remember

always that I am joyful

because of you. Amen.

God,

I feel like I've been kicked in
the stomach. I am breathless
with grief. I am beyond sad; I
am numb. Don't leave me
like this, O God. Breathe
your Spirit upon me and let
me live again. Amen.

God,

I'm so angry I can't see
straight. Keep me from doing
something I'll live to regret.
Protect me from myself right
now, and guard me until I've
calmed down. Amen.

God,

There is a hole in my life

today. I deeply miss

_____. Bless to me your

presence and let me feel the

touch of your love, for I am

in sore need of you. Amen.

God,

Why have you taken

_____ away from me?

I'm hurt and angry, and I feel

so alone. Please help me. Do

something. I can't see my

loved one, but let me see you

today. Amen.

God,

I am so sad. Let me cling to
you today like a child clings
to her mother. Let me know
the power of your love and
the force of your life. Amen.

God,

I am breathless with pain.

You are the God of Life. In

you is light and there is no

darkness at all. Help me hold

fast to my faith in spite of my

grief. I love you. Amen.